HOUGHTON MIFFLIN

Share

INVITATIONS
TO LITERACY

Houghton Mifflin Company • Boston

Atlanta • Dallas • Geneva, Illinois • Palo Alto • Princeton

HOUGHTON MIFFLIN

Share

Senior Authors

J. David Cooper
John J. Pikulski

Authors

Kathryn H. Au
Margarita Calderón
Jacqueline C. Comas
Marjorie Y. Lipson
J. Sabrina Mims
Susan E. Page
Sheila W. Valencia
MaryEllen Vogt

Consultants

Dolores Malcolm
Tina Saldivar
Shane Templeton

INVITATIONS
TO LITERACY

Houghton Mifflin Company • Boston

Atlanta • Dallas • Geneva, Illinois • Palo Alto • Princeton

Cover and title page photography by Tim Turner.

Cover illustration from *Flower Garden* by Eve Bunting, illustrated by
Kathryn Hewitt. Illustration copyright © 1994 by Kathryn Hewitt.
Reprinted by permission of Harcourt Brace & Company.

Acknowledgments appear on page 206.

ISBN 0-395-91479-5

789-VH-04 03 02 01 00 99

Getting Started

Themes

Sharing Time

BIG BOOK **PLUS**

CONTENTS

Creepy Crawlies

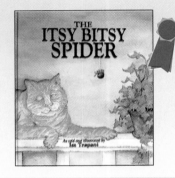

Meet Taro Gomi

Taro Gomi didn't like art when he was young. He says, "I was just a little naughty boy." Later, Mr. Gomi learned to draw and write books. Now he likes to learn new things, just like the girl in *My Friends*. So far, he's learned how to ski, cook, and play tennis.

11

I learned to walk from my friend
the cat.

I learned to jump from my friend
the dog.

I learned to climb from my friend
the monkey.

I learned to run from my friend
the horse.

20

I learned to march from my friend
the rooster.

I learned to nap from

my friend the crocodile.

I learned to smell the flowers
from my friend the butterfly.

I learned to hide from

my friend the rabbit.

I learned to explore the earth from

my friend the ant.

I learned to kick from my friend
the gorilla.

I learned to watch the night sky
from my friend the owl.

I learned to sing from my friends the birds.

I learned to read from

my friends the books.

I learned to study from

my friends the teachers.

I learned to play from

my friends at school.

And I learned to love from a friend like you.

YOU'RE THE TEACHER

The girl in the story had friends who taught her things. You can be a teacher, too! Show a friend how to do something you've learned.

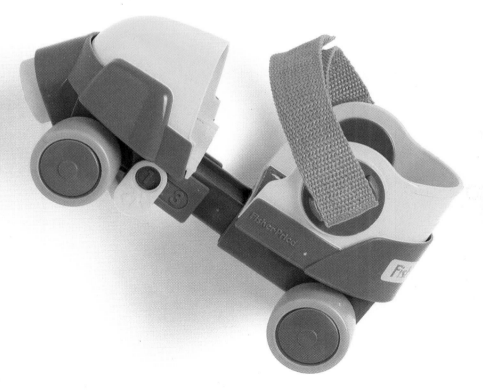

43

Sharing Time

The Doorbell Rang
by Pat Hutchins

The Doorbell Rang
by Pat Hutchins

llama

turtle

octo

Table of Contents

More Books You Can Read!

PHONICS BOOKSHELF
The Fans

PHONICS BOOKSHELF
Let Ben Help

PHONICS BOOKSHELF
The Hot Spot

WATCH **ME** READ
I Like Cats

WATCH **ME** READ
A Big Help

WATCH **ME** READ
Great Frogs!

PAPERBACK **PLUS**

Meet Byron Barton

Byron Barton was born in Rhode Island. He says, "To a small boy, our home with its woodpiles, barns, and attics made an ideal playground." Mr. Barton also loved to draw as a boy. He has written and illustrated many books.

Once there were four friends —

a pig,
a duck,

a cat,

and a little red hen.

The little red hen had three baby chicks.

One day the little red hen was pecking in the ground,

52

and she found some seeds.

She went to her three friends and asked,
"Who will help me plant these seeds?"

"Not I," squealed the pig.
"Not I," quacked the duck.
"Not I," meowed the cat.

"Then I will plant the seeds," said the little red hen.
And she did.

And the seeds sprouted and grew into
large stalks of wheat.

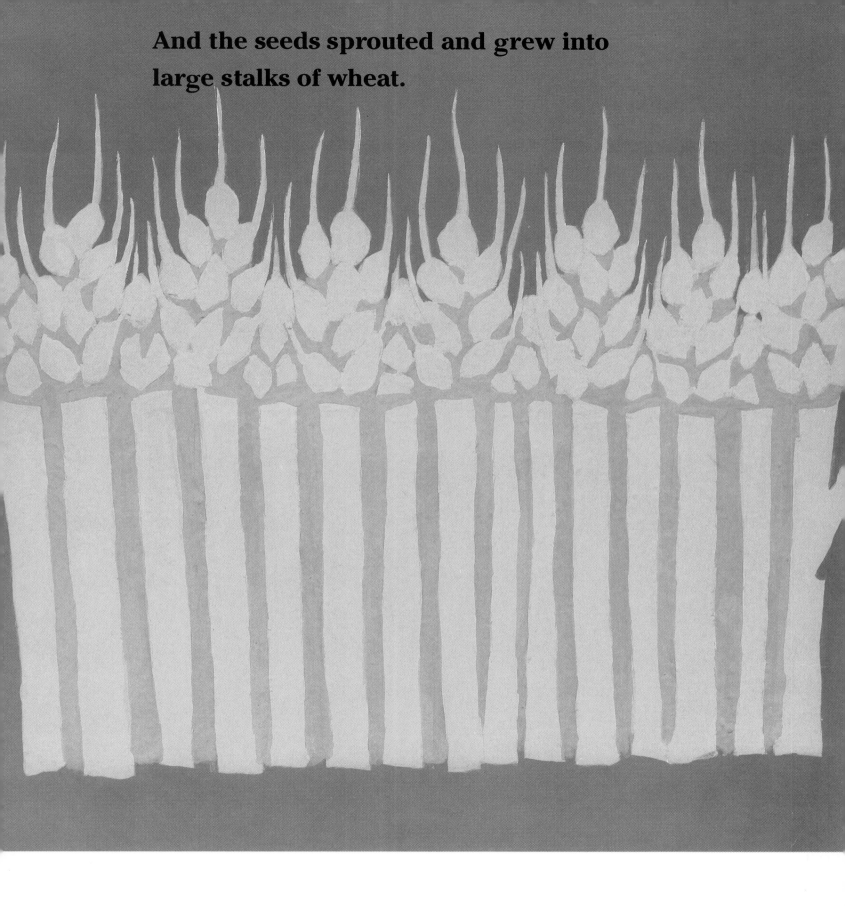

Then the little red hen asked her three friends,
"Who will help me cut these stalks of wheat?"

"Not I," meowed the cat.
"Not I," squealed the pig.
"Not I," quacked the duck.

59

"Then I will cut the wheat," said the little red hen.

And she did.

Then the little red hen asked her friends,
"Who will help me thresh this wheat?"

"Not I," squealed the pig.   "Not I," quacked the duck.

"Not I," meowed the cat.

"Then I will thresh the wheat," said the little red hen.

And she did.

Then the little red hen asked her friends,
"Who will help me grind these grains of wheat into flour?"

"Not I," squealed the pig.
"Not I," quacked the duck.
"Not I," meowed the cat.

"Then I will grind the wheat into flour,"
said the little red hen.

And she did.

Then the little red hen asked her three friends,
"Who will help me make this flour into bread?"

"Not I," meowed the cat.
"Not I," squealed the pig.
"Not I," quacked the duck.

"Then I will make the flour into bread," she said.

And she did.

Then the little red hen called to her friends,
"Who will help me eat   this bread?"

"I will," quacked the duck.
"I will," meowed the cat.
"I will," squealed the pig.

"Oh no," said the little red hen.

"We will eat the bread."

And they did —

the little red hen and her three little chicks.

It's Showtime!

Make animal puppets. Use your
puppets to act out *The Little Red Hen*!

The Sharing Song

a song by Raffi

It's mine, but you can have some,
With you I'd like to share it,
'Cause if I share it with you
You'll have some too.

Well, if I have a cake to eat,
If I have a tasty treat,
If you come to me and ask,
I'll give some to you.

Well, if I have a book to read,
If I have a block you need,
If you come to me and ask
I'll share it with you.

82

My Mami Takes Me to the Bakery
by *Charlotte Pomerantz*

Let's buy pan de agua, daughter.

Pan is bread and agua, water.

Good fresh bread of flour and water.

Good fresh pan de agua, daughter.

Inside the panadería,

There's the hot sweet smell of pan.

Good day, says the plump panadero.

(The baker's a very nice man.)

84

How many loaves, Señora, he asks:

Uno...dos?

Dos? Sí, sí.

Two, por favor, says my mami

Two loaves for my daughter and me.

85

Sharing Stories
from Long Ago

Len Cabral is a storyteller. Here he is telling "Anansi's Narrow Waist," a West African folktale. People have been telling this story for hundreds of years.

Your Turn!

Anyone who knows a story can be a storyteller. This girl is telling one of her favorite fairy tales. Can you guess what story she is telling?

Now it's your turn. Tell a story to your friends!

Together

by Paul Engle

Because we do
All things together
All things improve,
Even weather.

Our daily meat
And bread taste better,
Trees are greener,
Rain is wetter.

89

Meet Eve Bunting

Eve Bunting was born in Ireland. She grew up listening to folktales and has loved storytelling ever since. Ms. Bunting says, "For me, writing is like breathing." She has written over one hundred books for children.

Meet Kathryn Hewitt

Kathryn Hewitt is an artist and a teacher. When not working, she enjoys being with her children and their nine pets. Ms. Hewitt says, "I play and read with my family as often as possible."

EVE BUNTING

Flower Garden

ILLUSTRATED BY KATHRYN HEWITT

Garden in a shopping cart
Doesn't it look great?

Garden on the checkout stand
I can hardly wait.

Garden in a cardboard box
Walking to the bus

Garden sitting on our laps
People smile at us!

Garden going up the stairs
Stopping at each floor

This garden's getting heavier!
At last — our own front door.

Hurry! Hurry! Get the trowel
Spread the papers thick.

Get the bag of potting soil
Get the planting mix.

Put purple
pansies at
each end

Daisies, white
as snow

Daffodils, and tulips
geraniums in a row.

Garden in a window box
High above the street

Where butterflies
can stop and rest
And ladybugs can meet.

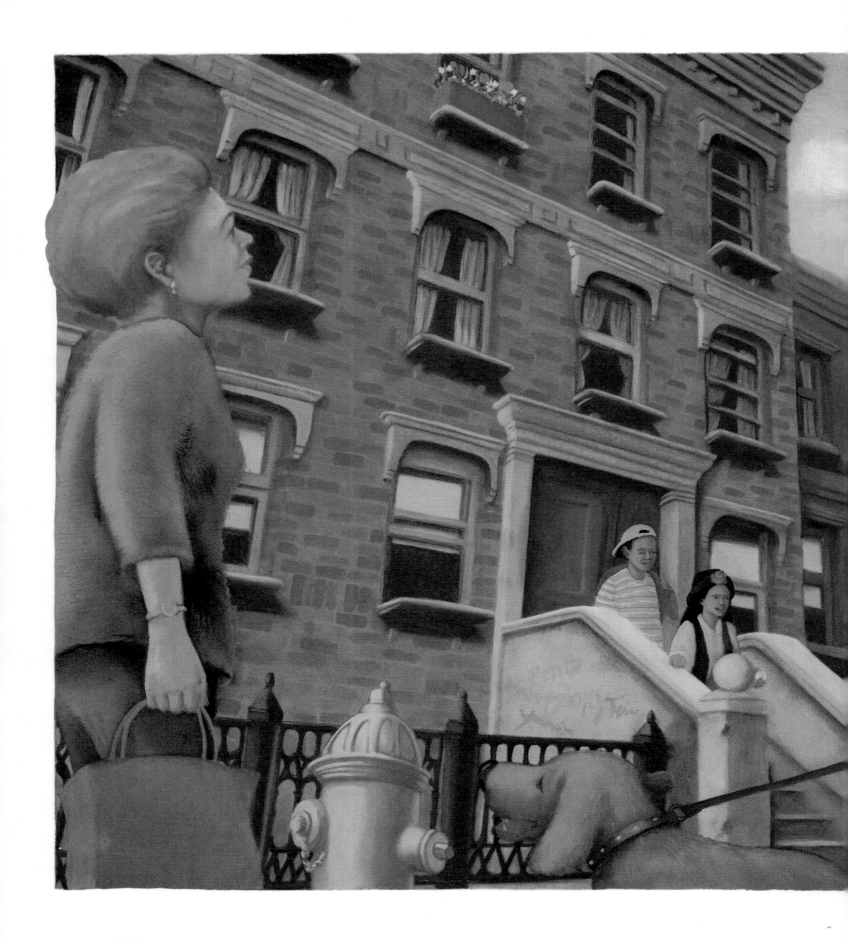

Walkers walking down below
Will lift their heads and see
Purple, yellow, red, and white
A color jamboree.

Candles on a birthday cake
Chocolate ice cream, too.

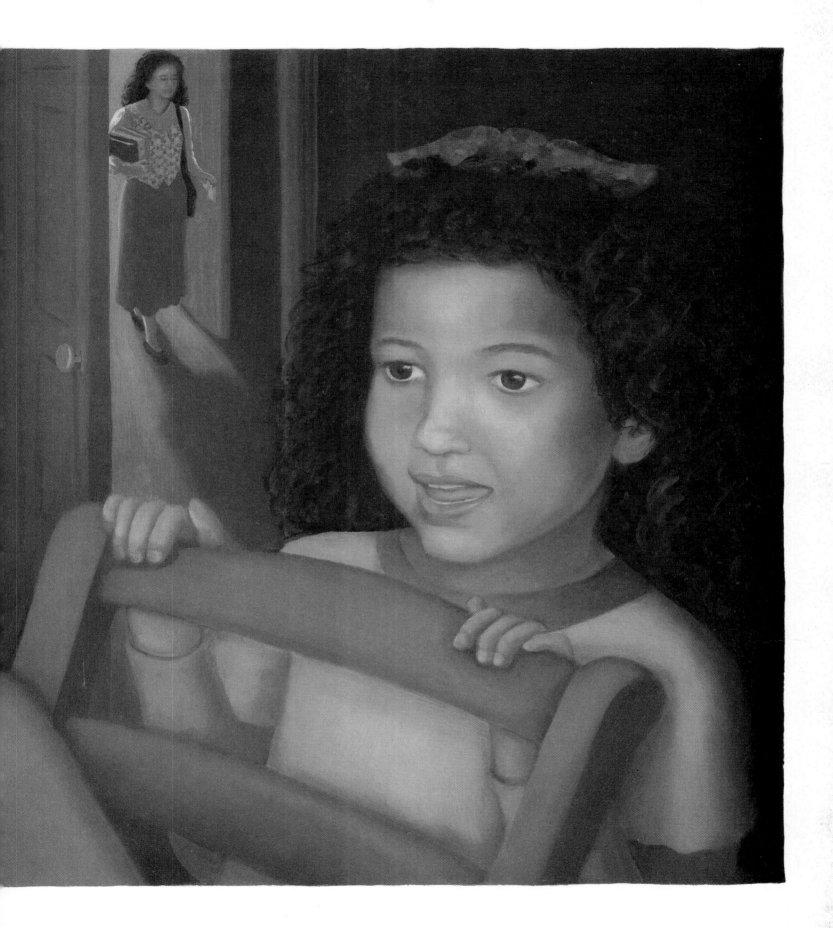

Happy, happy birthday, Mom!
A garden box — for you.

A Window Box to Share

You can make a window box too. Use tissue paper for the flowers and a milk carton for the box. Share your window box with a friend!

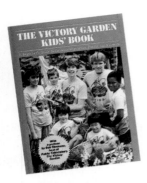

Growing a Victory Garden

The kids in the Kids' Victory Garden were all beginners. They came because it sounded like fun.

| May | July | August | November |

The kids learned to grow a garden from start to finish. This is how the garden looked.

Getting Started

You can start your garden in the spring, as soon as the soil is dry enough. Here are some things the kids did to get the garden ready.

Ben taking a wheelbarrow to the compost pile

Sarah choosing a package of seeds

Joe and Ben buying seedlings

Taking Care of the Garden

When it's time to take care of the garden, everyone shares the work.

Julie cutting yellow leaves off her parsley seedlings before planting

Sarah, Julie, and Ben at work on the scarecrow

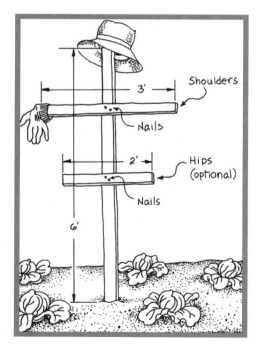

A drawing of the scarecrow

Sharing the Harvest

Sarah with a slippery watermelon

Finally it's time to harvest the garden. Sometimes you can just use your hands to pick the crops.

Joe about to harvest a cabbage

You can give some of your crops away . . . or you can share them with your friends!

Join the Band!

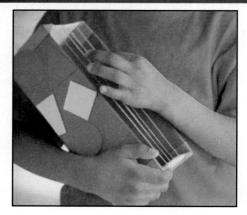

You and your friends can get together and share some beautiful music.

Shoebox Banjo

What You Need:

- a shoebox
- four rubber bands

What You Do:

1. First, cut small slits on two sides of the box.
2. Next, put the rubber bands around the box so that they fit into the slits.
3. Last, play the banjo with your fingers or with a small stick.

Oatmeal Box Drum

What You Need:

- an empty oatmeal box with the lid
- two unsharpened pencils

What You Do:

1. First, decorate your box.
2. Next, bang the box with your pencils.
3. Last, keep the beat for the band!

Humming Comb

What You Need:

- a comb
- a piece of waxed paper

What You Do:

1. First, fold the waxed paper in half. Put the teeth of the comb in the fold.
2. Next, hold the comb so that it is covered tightly with the paper.
3. Then put your lips over the paper.
4. Last, hum a tune!

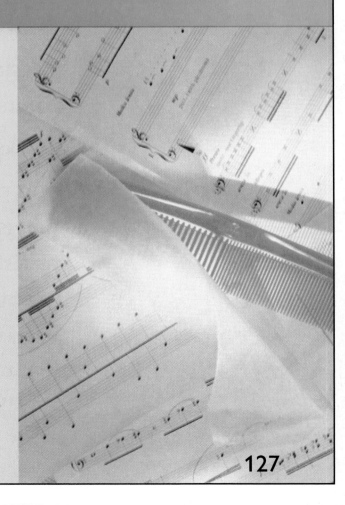

127

How to Make a Fishing Pole

Instructions
by Brent Spenser Marcinek

Brent wanted to share something he knows how to do. Find out from him how to make a fishing pole.

Brent Spenser Marcinek
Cassidy Elementary School
Lexington, Kentucky

Brent enjoys baseball, football, and playing with his iguana. When he visits his grandmother, he likes to fish in the lake behind her house. Brent likes fishing with his Uncle Van, who helped him make a fishing pole.

128

How to Make a Fishing Pole

First, you get a stick. Then you get some fishing line, and you tie the fishing line on the stick. Last, you get your mom or dad to get a hook and tie it.

You Can Make a Difference!

Here are some good ways to share and to help others.

1 Make conservation posters.

Let people know how they can help take care of our planet.

2 Donate old books.

If you've finished reading it, share it with someone else.

3 Make a coloring book.

Draw pictures you can bind into a book for a younger kid to color.

Selection from *Nickelodeon's The Big Help Book,* by Alan Goodman.
Illustrations by Fiona Smith. Copyright © 1994 by Nickelodeon.
Reprinted by permission. All rights reserved.

130

5

Send cards to a hospital pen pal.

People in the hospital like to get mail. Your pictures might even help someone get better!

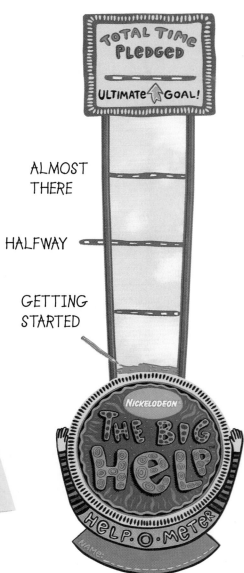

TOTAL TIME PLEDGED

ULTIMATE GOAL!

ALMOST THERE

HALFWAY

GETTING STARTED

NICKELODEON

THE BIG HELP

HELP·O·METER

NAME:

Dear Mrs. Lucas,
This is a picture of my new puppy. I hope it cheers you up!

Jackie

4

Read to someone who can no longer see well.

People with trouble reading still like books and stories. They just need someone else to read to them.

Keep track of every hour that you spend helping. You'll see what a difference you're making!

131

Main aux Fleurs (Hand with Flowers)

by Pablo Picasso

Flowers

Flowers grow in the meadow
and friendships grow in your heart.

Butterflies fly in the meadow
where the flowers grow.
Love flies in your heart
where friendships grow.

by Amanda Venta, Age 6

Creepy Crawlies

The Itsy Bitsy Spider
by Iza Trapani

Table of Contents

More Books You Can Read!

WONDERFUL WORMS

PAPERBACK **PLUS**

BY LINDA GLASER
PICTURES BY LORETTA KRUPINSKI

PHONICS BOOKSHELF

The Big
Dig

PHONICS BOOKSHELF

Bug and
Slug

PHONICS BOOKSHELF

The Other
Side of Bugs

WATCH **ME** READ

Try, Try
Again

WATCH **ME** READ

Grasshopper
and Ant

WATCH **ME** READ

All in
Fun

Ask Eric Carle

How did you come up with the idea for _The Very Hungry Caterpillar_?

One day, over 25 years ago, I was punching holes in a stack of paper. Looking at the holes, I thought of a bookworm. Later, the bookworm became a caterpillar. And that was the beginning!

What is your favorite book?

My favorite book is _Do You Want to Be My Friend?_ because it's about friendship.

THE VERY HUNGRY CATERPILLAR

by Eric Carle

In the light of the moon
a little egg lay on a leaf.

141

One Sunday morning the warm sun came up
and — pop! — out of the egg came a tiny and
very hungry caterpillar.

He started to look for some food.

On Monday he ate through one apple.
But he was still hungry.

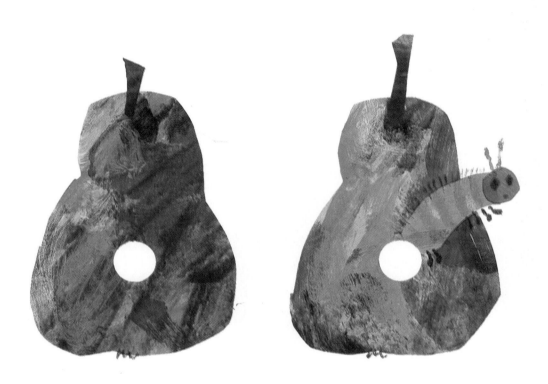

On Tuesday he ate through two pears,
but he was still hungry.

On Wednesday he ate through three plums,
but he was still hungry.

On Thursday he ate through four strawberries,
but he was still hungry.

On Friday he ate through five oranges,

but he was still hungry.

On Saturday he ate through

one piece of
chocolate cake,

one pickle,

one ice-cream cone,

one slice of
Swiss cheese,

one slice of salami,

one sausage,

one piece of
cherry pie,

one lollipop,

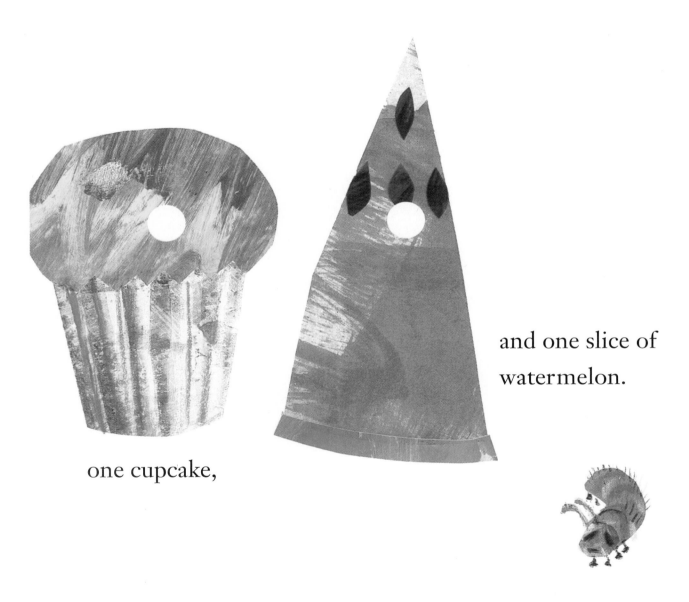

one cupcake,

and one slice of
watermelon.

That night he had a stomachache!

The next day was Sunday again.

The caterpillar ate through
one nice green leaf, and after
that he felt much better.

Now he wasn't hungry
any more — and he wasn't
a little caterpillar any more.
He was a big, fat caterpillar.

He built a small house, called a cocoon,
around himself. He stayed inside
for more than two weeks. Then he
nibbled a hole in the cocoon, pushed
his way out and . . .

he was a beautiful butterfly!

Make a Get-Well Card

Caterpillar did not feel well after he ate all that food! Write a get-well card to make him feel better.

Get well soon

Dear Caterpillar,

Get Well, Caterpillar

Dear Caterpillar,

Feel better soon!

CREEPY CRAWLY POEMS

illustrated by Eric Carle

The face of the dragonfly
Is practically nothing
But eyes.

Haiku by Chisoku

MY OPINION

Is a caterpillar ticklish?
Well, it's always my belief
That he giggles as he wiggles
Across a hairy leaf.

by Monica Shannon

BE AN ARTIST

The steps on the next page tell how to make a **collage**. You might want to make your own caterpillar.

"It's messy, but fun," Eric Carle says.

LIKE ERIC CARLE

1 Paint several pieces of paper. Let them dry.

2 Draw outlines on the paper.

3 Cut out the shapes. You might want to make a face!

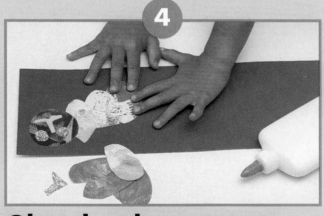

4 Glue the shapes on a page.

Jima the Worm and the Perfect House

A Story by Joanna Ruth Miller

Can Jima the worm find the perfect house?
Read Joanna's story and find out!

Joanna Ruth Miller
Detroit, Michigan

Joanna was seven years old when she wrote this story. She likes worms, other creepy crawlies, and reading. Jima is the name of Joanna's baby sitter.

Jima the Worm and the Perfect House

Jima was a little gray worm with blue eyes. He lived on a grassy hill. He loved to wiggle in the dirt with his friends Tommy and Katy.

One rainy day, Jima was in his house. He felt a drop of water on his tail. Water dripped all over the place. There was so much water that he had to move.

First he found a large apple. He munched through it. It was a good snack but not a very good house. This was not the perfect house.

167

Next he found an old eggshell. It was too small. This was not the perfect house.

Then he found a rotten orange. It was too mushy. This was not the perfect house.

Then Tommy and Katy saw Jima. "I can't find the perfect house," Jima said.

"Why don't you go back to your old house?" Tommy said.

"No, my house has a leak," Jima said.

"We'll help you fix it,"
Katy and Tommy said. They all
wiggled to Jima's house. The
leak was not there anymore!

"This is the perfect house!"
Jima said.

Butterfly ABC

What letters do you see on these butterfly wings?

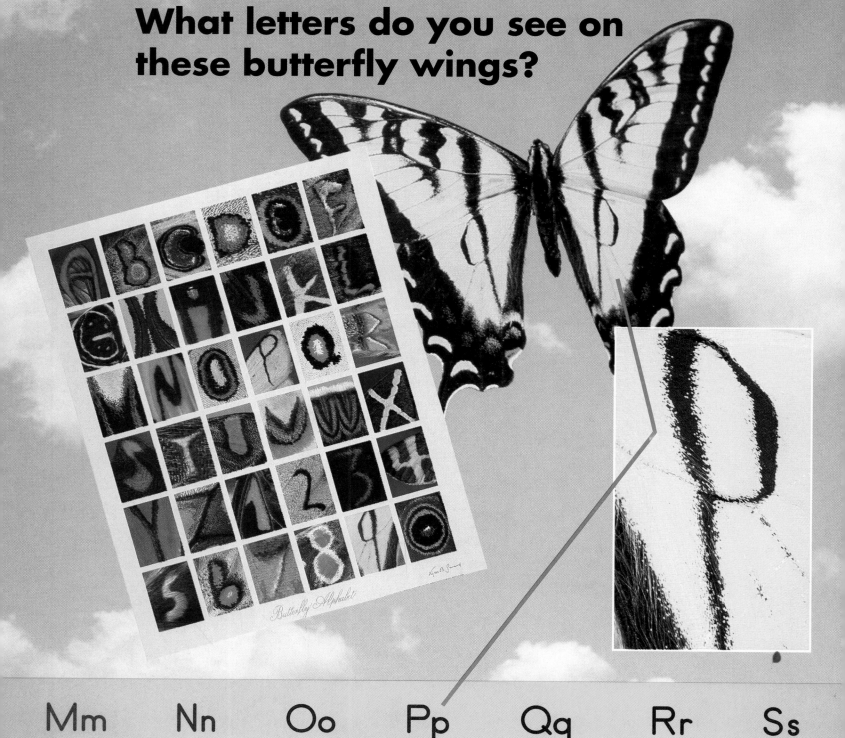

Aa   Bb   Cc   Dd   Ee   Ff

Mm   Nn   Oo   Pp   Qq   Rr   Ss

Butterfly Alphabet

Gg Hh Ii Jj Kk Ll

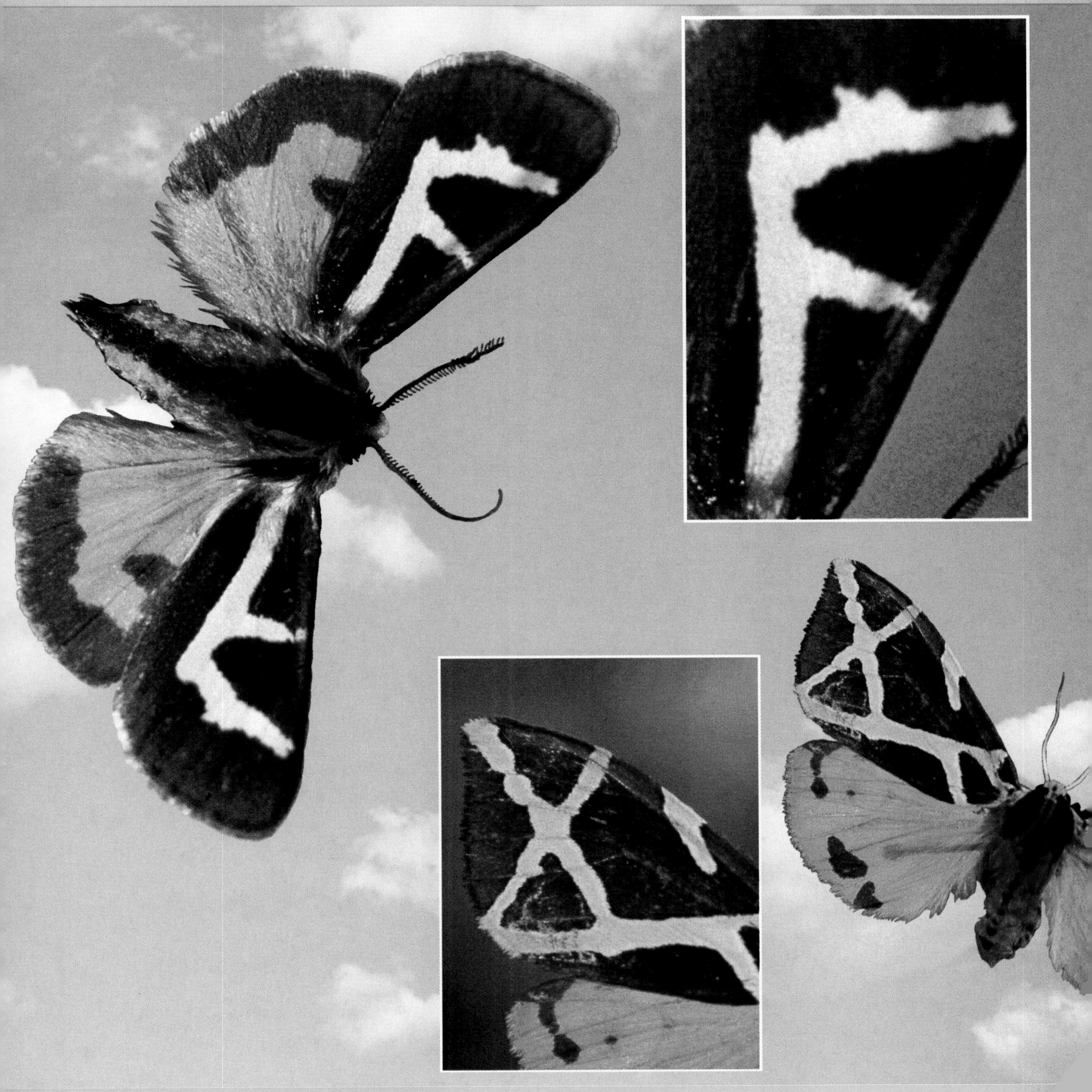

Tt Uu Vv Ww Xx Yy Zz

Meet
Leo Lionni

When Leo Lionni was a boy, he loved to study nature and art. He collected and drew plants, shells, stones, and leaves. Many of his books show the things he liked to collect.

Leo Lionni

A Color of His Own

Parrots are green

goldfish are red

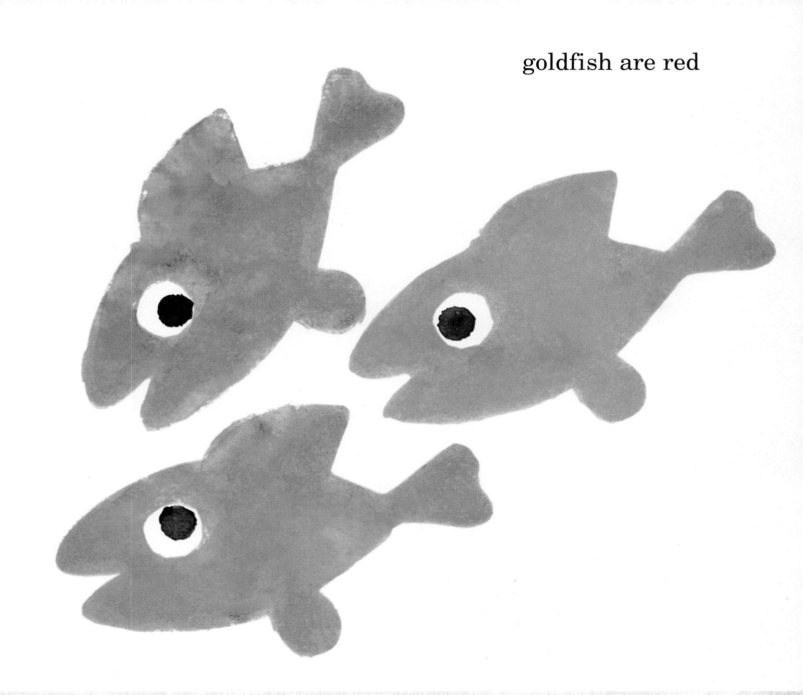

elephants are gray

pigs are pink.

All animals have a color of their own –

except for chameleons.

They change color wherever they go.

On lemons they are yellow.

In the heather they are purple.

And on the tiger they are striped
like tigers.

One day a chameleon
who was sitting
on a tiger's tail
said to himself,

"If I remain on a leaf,
I shall be green forever,
and so I too will have
a color of my own."

With this thought he cheerfully climbed
onto the greenest leaf.

But in autumn the leaf turned yellow
— and so did the chameleon.

Later the leaf turned red,
and the chameleon too turned red.

And then
the winter winds
blew the leaf from
the branch
and with it
the chameleon.

The chameleon was black in the long winter night.

But when spring came, he walked out
into the green grass.
And there he met another chameleon.

He told his sad story.
"Won't we ever have a color
of our own?" he asked.

"I'm afraid not," said the other chameleon,
who was older and wiser.
"But," he added,
"why don't we stay together?

"We will still change color
wherever we go,
but you and I
will always be alike."

And so they remained side by side.

They were green together

and purple

and yellow

and red with white polka dots. And they lived happily

ever after.

LET'S COUNT!

Our Favorite Chameleons

Vote for your favorite color chameleon from the story. Make a chart to show which color chameleon is the class favorite.

The Chameleon

People say the Chameleon
    can take on the hue
Of whatever he happens to be on.
    It's true —
Within reason, of course. If you
    put him on plaid
Or polka dots, he really gets mad.

by John Gardner

Creepy Crawly Facts

chameleon

A chameleon can use its long tail to hang on a branch like a monkey.

You can tell this frog is poisonous by its red color.

poison arrow frog

praying mantis

A mantis uses its legs as a toothbrush.

ACKNOWLEDGMENTS

For each of the selections listed below, grateful acknowledgment is made for permission to excerpt and/or reprint original or copyrighted material, as follows:

Selections

A Color of His Own, by Leo Lionni. Copyright © 1975 by Leo Lionni. Reprinted by permission of Alfred A. Knopf, a division of Random House, Inc.

Flower Garden, by Eve Bunting. Text copyright © 1994 by Eve Bunting. Illustrations copyright © 1994 by Kathryn Hewitt. Reprinted by permission of Harcourt Brace & Company.

"Join the Band," from June 1994 *Sesame Street Magazine*. Copyright © 1994 by Children's Television Workshop. Reprinted by permission.

The Little Red Hen, by Byron Barton. Copyright © 1993 by Byron Barton. Reprinted by permission of HarperCollins Publishers.

My Friends, by Taro Gomi. Copyright © 1989 by Taro Gomi. English text copyright © 1990 by Chronicle Books. Reprinted by permission of Chronicle Books.

Selection from *Nickelodeon's The Big Help Book,* by Alan Goodman. Illustrations by Fiona Smyth. Copyright © 1994 by Nickelodeon. Reprinted by permission. All rights reserved.

The Very Hungry Caterpillar, by Eric Carle. Copyright © 1969 by Eric Carle. Reprinted by permission of Philomel Books.

The Victory Garden Kids' Book, by Marjorie Waters, illustrated by George Ulrich. Copyright © 1988 by Marjorie Waters and WGBH Educational Foundation. Reprinted by permission of Globe Pequot Press.

Poetry

"The Chameleon," by John Gardner, from *A Child's Bestiary*. Copyright © 1975 by Boskydell Artists. Reprinted by permission of Georges Borchardt, Inc. for the Estate of John Gardner.

"the face of a dragonfly," by Chisoku, from *Haiku* Vols. i-iv, edited and translated by R. H. Blyth. Reprinted by permission of The Hokuseido Press Co., Ltd. Dragonfly illustration by Eric Carle, from *Animals, Animals.* Copyright © 1989 by Eric Carle. Reprinted by permission of Philomel Books.

"Flowers," by Amanda Venta, from June 1994 *Highlights for Children* magazine. Copyright © 1994 by Highlights for Children, Inc., Columbus, Ohio. Reprinted by permission of the author and Highlights for Children, Inc.

"My Mami Takes Me to the Bakery," from *The Tamarindo Puppy and Other Poems,* by Charlotte Pomerantz. Copyright © 1980 by Charlotte Pomerantz. Reprinted by permission of Greenwillow Books, a division of William Morrow & Company, Inc.

"My Opinion," from *Goose Grass Rhymes*, by Monica Shannon. Copyright © 1930 by Doubleday, a division of Bantam, Doubleday, Dell Publishing Group, Inc. Reprinted by permission. Caterpillar illustration, by Eric Carle, from *Animals, Animals.* Copyright © 1989 by Eric Carle. Reprinted by permission of Philomel Books.

"The Sharing Song," music by Raffi, words by Raffi, D. Pike, and B. & B. Simpson. Copyright © 1976 by Homeland Publishing, a division of Troubadour Records Ltd. Reprinted by permission of Troubadour Records Ltd.

"Together," from *Embrace: Selected Love Poems,* by Paul Engle. Copyright © 1969 by Paul Engle. Reprinted by permission of Random House, Inc.

Special thanks to the following teachers whose students' compositions appear in the Be a Writer and Be an Artist features in this level: Mary Parks, Naperville, Illinois; Allyn Schrader, Cassidy Elementary School, Lexington, Kentucky.

CREDITS

Illustration **11** (inset), **5, 12–42** Taro Gomi; **6** (top), **46** Pat Hutchins; **7, 47** Vivi Escrivá; **2** (left), **6, 49–78** Byron Barton; **83–85** Gerardo Suzan; **7, 91–120** Kathryn Hewitt; **129** Brent Marcinek; **7, 130** Fiona Smyth; **8, 136** Iza Trapani; **9, 137** Loretta Krupinski; **2** (bottom), **8, 139–161, 163** Eric Carle; **169** Joanna Ruth Miller; **1, 2** (right center), **9, 173–201** Leo Lionni

Assignment Photography **128–129** (background) Banta Digital Group; **86–87** Kindra Clineff; **158** (bottom), **159** (insets), Lou Jones; **10–11, 43, 44–47, 48–49** (background), **80–82** (borders), **90–91** (background), **121** (background), **134–135, 138–139** (border), **140–141, 158–159** (border), **204–205** (border) Tony Scarpetta; **44–47, 130–131, 135** (inset), **162, 170,** Tracey Wheeler

Photography 2 © Gary Mottau / Landwerk (tl) **10** Naka Ochiaiz / Chronical Books **43** David Grossman / Photoresearchers (t); Jose Pelgez / The Stock Market (b); J.Pinderhughes / The Stock Market (m) **48** Courtesy of Byron Barton **88** Grant V. Faint / The Image Bank (tl) **88** © Rod Currie / © Tony Stone Images / Chicago Inc. (l); Jeffery W. Myers / The Stock Market (ml); P. Dawlat / Photo Researchers (br) **89** © Erika Stone / Photo Researchers (tl); © Ben Mitchell / The Image Bank (tr); © Randy Wells / © Tony Stone Images/Chicago Inc. (r); Patti & Mike Putnam / The Stock Market (br) **90** Courtesy of Eve Bunting (tl); Courtesy of Kathryn Hewitt (br); **122–125** © Gary Motteau / Landwerk **126** Dennis Mosner **128** Courtesy of Brent Spenser Marcinek **132** (c) 1996 Artist's Rights Society (ARS) New York/Spadem, Paris **134** Animals Animals (t); D.R. Specker / Animals Animals (l) **135** Allstock (t); © Kjell B. Sandved / Sandved Photography (b) **138** © Sigrid Estrada (inset) **164** © Sigred Estrada (inset) **166** Courtesy of Joanna Ruth Miller (inset) **170–171** John Banagan / The Image Bank (background) **170** © Kjell B. Sandved / Sandved Photography (l, m, r) **171** © Kjell B. Sandved / Sandved Photography (tr, r, b, br) **172** Massimo Pacifico / Random House (inset) **203** © Art Wolfe (tl); Michael Fogdon /DRK Photo (tr); Art Wolfe / © Tony Stone Images/ Chicago Inc. (bl); © Art Wolfe (br) **204** Martin Harvey / The Wildlife Collection **205** Kenneth Deitcher / The Wildlife Collection (t); Robert Parks / The Wildlife Collection (b)

Kids' Clubhouse

Here's what visitors to our Web site said about stories in *Share.*

Flower Garden was great. I loved the part when the little girl brought the flowers home for her mother's birthday. I liked when she picked out all the flowers she wanted. And I knew all the flowers she picked out.

Justin Toran-Burrell, Massachusetts

The Very Hungry Caterpillar was a cool book. He ate like a pig. He ate more than me. He had a stomachache that night. This was my favorite part because he had a funny look on his head.

Denise Robinson, Maine

Post your reviews in the

Kids' Clubhouse

at

www.eduplace.com